2016 SQA Past Papers With Answers

GW00771662

Higher
SPANISH

FREE
audio files to accompany this title can be
accessed at
www.hoddergibson.co.uk
• Click on the turquoise 'Updates and Extras' box.
• Look for the 'SQA Papers Audio Files' heading
and click the 'Browse' button beneath.
• You will then find the files listed
by language and level.

2014 Specimen Question Paper, 2015 & 2016 Exams

HODDER
GIBSON
AN HACHETTE UK COMPANY

This book contains the official 2014 SQA Specimen Question Paper, 2015 and 2016 Exams for Higher Spanish, with associated SQA-approved answers modified from the official marking instructions that accompany the paper.

In addition the book contains study skills advice. This advice has been specially commissioned by Hodder Gibson, and has been written by experienced senior teachers and examiners in line with the new Higher for CfE syllabus and assessment outlines. This is not SQA material but has been devised to provide further practice for Higher examinations.

Hodder Gibson is grateful to the copyright holders, as credited on the final page of the Answer Section, for permission to use their material. Every effort has been made to trace the copyright holders and to obtain their permission for the use of copyright material. Hodder Gibson will be happy to receive information allowing us to rectify any error or omission in future editions.

Hachette UK's policy is to use papers that are natural, renewable and recyclable products and made from wood grown in sustainable forests. The logging and manufacturing processes are expected to conform to the environmental regulations of the country of origin.

Orders: please contact Bookpoint Ltd, 130 Park Drive, Milton Park, Abingdon, Oxon, OX14 4SE. Telephone: (44) 01235 827720. Fax: (44) 01235 400454. Lines are open 9.00–5.00, Monday to Saturday, with a 24-hour message answering service. Visit our website at www.hoddereducation.co.uk. Hodder Gibson can be contacted direct on: Tel: 0141 333 4650; Fax: 0141 404 8188; email: hoddergibson@hodder.co.uk

This collection first published in 2016 by
Hodder Gibson, an imprint of Hodder Education,
An Hachette UK Company
211 St Vincent Street
Glasgow G2 5QY

Typeset by Aptara, Inc.

Printed in the UK

A catalogue record for this title is available from the British Library

ISBN: 978-1-4718-9101-4

3 2 1

2017 2016

Introduction

Study Skills – what you need to know to pass exams!

Pause for thought

Many students might skip quickly through a page like this. After all, we all know how to revise. Do you really though?

Think about this:

"IF YOU ALWAYS DO WHAT YOU ALWAYS DO, YOU WILL ALWAYS GET WHAT YOU HAVE ALWAYS GOT."

Do you like the grades you get? Do you want to do better? If you get full marks in your assessment, then that's great! Change nothing! This section is just to help you get that little bit better than you already are.

There are two main parts to the advice on offer here. The first part highlights fairly obvious things but which are also very important. The second part makes suggestions about revision that you might not have thought about but which WILL help you.

Part 1

DOH! It's so obvious but …

Start revising in good time

Don't leave it until the last minute – this will make you panic.

Make a revision timetable that sets out work time AND play time.

Sleep and eat!

Obvious really, and very helpful. Avoid arguments or stressful things too – even games that wind you up. You need to be fit, awake and focused!

Know your place!

Make sure you know exactly **WHEN and WHERE** your exams are.

Know your enemy!

Make sure you know what to expect in the exam.

How is the paper structured?

How much time is there for each question?

What types of question are involved?

Which topics seem to come up time and time again?

Which topics are your strongest and which are your weakest?

Are all topics compulsory or are there choices?

Learn by DOING!

There is no substitute for past papers and practice papers – they are simply essential! Tackling this collection of papers and answers is exactly the right thing to be doing as your exams approach.

Part 2

People learn in different ways. Some like low light, some bright. Some like early morning, some like evening / night. Some prefer warm, some prefer cold. But everyone uses their BRAIN and the brain works when it is active. Passive learning – sitting gazing at notes – is the most INEFFICIENT way to learn anything. Below you will find tips and ideas for making your revision more effective and maybe even more enjoyable. What follows gets your brain active, and active learning works!

Activity 1 – Stop and review

Step 1

When you have done no more than 5 minutes of revision reading STOP!

Step 2

Write a heading in your own words which sums up the topic you have been revising.

Step 3

Write a summary of what you have revised in no more than two sentences. Don't fool yourself by saying, "I know it, but I cannot put it into words". That just means you don't know it well enough. If you cannot write your summary, revise that section again, knowing that you must write a summary at the end of it. Many of you will have notebooks full of blue/black ink writing. Many of the pages will not be especially attractive or memorable so try to liven them up a bit with colour as you are reviewing and rewriting. **This is a great memory aid, and memory is the most important thing.**

Activity 2 – Use technology!

Why should everything be written down? Have you thought about "mental" maps, diagrams, cartoons and colour to help you learn? And rather than write down notes, why not record your revision material?

What about having a text message revision session with friends? Keep in touch with them to find out how and what they are revising and share ideas and questions.

Why not make a video diary where you tell the camera what you are doing, what you think you have learned and what you still have to do? No one has to see or hear it, but the process of having to organise your thoughts in a formal way to explain something is a very important learning practice.

Be sure to make use of electronic files. You could begin to summarise your class notes. Your typing might be slow, but it will get faster and the typed notes will be easier to read than the scribbles in your class notes. Try to add different fonts and colours to make your work stand out. You can easily Google relevant pictures, cartoons and diagrams which you can copy and paste to make your work more attractive and **MEMORABLE**.

Activity 3 – This is it. Do this and you will know lots!

Step 1

In this task you must be very honest with yourself! Find the SQA syllabus for your subject (www.sqa.org.uk). Look at how it is broken down into main topics called MANDATORY knowledge. That means stuff you MUST know.

Step 2

BEFORE you do ANY revision on this topic, write a list of everything that you already know about the subject. It might be quite a long list but you only need to write it once. It shows you all the information that is already in your long-term memory so you know what parts you do not need to revise!

Step 3

Pick a chapter or section from your book or revision notes. Choose a fairly large section or a whole chapter to get the most out of this activity.

With a buddy, use Skype, Facetime, Twitter or any other communication you have, to play the game "If this is the answer, what is the question?". For example, if you are revising Geography and the answer you provide is "meander", your buddy would have to make up a question like "What is the word that describes a feature of a river where it flows slowly and bends often from side to side?".

Make up 10 "answers" based on the content of the chapter or section you are using. Give this to your buddy to solve while you solve theirs.

Step 4

Construct a wordsearch of at least 10 × 10 squares. You can make it as big as you like but keep it realistic. Work together with a group of friends. Many apps allow you to make wordsearch puzzles online. The words and phrases can go in any direction and phrases can be split. Your puzzle must only contain facts linked to the topic you are revising. Your task is to find 10 bits of information to hide in your puzzle, but you must not repeat information that you used in Step 3. DO NOT show where the words are. Fill up empty squares with random letters. Remember to keep a note of where your answers are hidden but do not show your friends. When you have a complete puzzle, exchange it with a friend to solve each other's puzzle.

Step 5

Now make up 10 questions (not "answers" this time) based on the same chapter used in the previous two tasks. Again, you must find NEW information that you have not yet used. Now it's getting hard to find that new information! Again, give your questions to a friend to answer.

Step 6

As you have been doing the puzzles, your brain has been actively searching for new information. Now write a NEW LIST that contains only the new information you have discovered when doing the puzzles. Your new list is the one to look at repeatedly for short bursts over the next few days. Try to remember more and more of it without looking at it. After a few days, you should be able to add words from your second list to your first list as you increase the information in your long-term memory.

FINALLY! Be inspired...

Make a list of different revision ideas and beside each one write **THINGS I HAVE** tried, **THINGS I WILL** try and **THINGS I MIGHT** try. Don't be scared of trying something new.

And remember – "FAIL TO PREPARE AND PREPARE TO FAIL!"

Higher Spanish

The course

The Higher Spanish course aims to enable you to develop the ability to:

- read, listen, talk and write in Spanish
- understand and use Spanish
- apply your knowledge and understanding of the language.

The course offers the opportunity to develop detailed language skills in the real-life contexts of society, learning, employability, and culture.

How the course is graded

The course assessment will take the form of a performance and a written exam.

- The performance will be a presentation and discussion with your teacher, which will be recorded and marked by your teacher. This is out of 30, and makes up 30% of your final mark.
- The written exam will be sat in May. This book will help you practise for the exam.

The exams

Reading and Directed Writing

- Exam time: 1 hour 40 minutes

Reading

- Total marks: 30
- Weighting in final grade: 30%
- What you have to do: read a passage of about 600 words, and answer questions about it in English, including an overall purpose question for 20 marks; then translate an extract from the passage of about 40 words into English for 10 marks.

Directed Writing

- Total marks: 10
- Weighting in final grade: 10%
- What you have to do: write 120–150 words in Spanish describing a visit you made, or an experience you had, in a Spanish speaking country.

Listening and Personal Response Writing

- Exam time: 60 minutes
- Total marks: 30
- Weighting in final grade: 30%
- What you have to do: Section 1 (20 marks): listen to a presentation in Spanish, and answer questions in English for 8 marks; then listen to a conversation in Spanish, and answer questions about it in English for 12 marks; Section 2 (10 marks): write 120–150 words in Spanish as a personal response to the topic discussed in the conversation: there will be three specific questions to be addressed. (Please note that SQA has decided that from 2017 onwards there won't be an overall purpose (tick box) question in the Listening Paper.)

How to improve your mark!

Reading

- Read the whole passage, then pick out the key points. Detailed answers are generally required, so pay particular attention to words like *tanto*, *muy*, *demasiado*, *un poco*, and to negatives. Make sure you get the details of numbers, days, times etc. right.
- Use the line numbers above each question to guide you as to where to look for the answer.
- Take care when using dictionaries where a word has more than one meaning. Learn to choose the correct meaning from a list of meanings in a dictionary, and get in the habit of going beyond the headword. Often you will find the whole phrase you are looking for further down the entry.
- Try to answer the specific wording of the question, but do not give a word-for-word translation of the text as a response to the reading comprehension questions, as this often results in an answer which is not in correct English.
- When responding to the questions in the Reading papers, you should be guided by the number of points awarded for each question. You should give as much detail in your answer as you have understood, but should not put down everything which is in the original text, as you are wasting time. The question itself usually indicates the amount of information required by stating in bold, e.g. "State **two** of them". If the question says "Give **any** two", there are more than two possibilities, so choose the two you are happiest with and stick to them.
- The final question before the translation asks you to look at the passage as a whole, then answer a question and provide evidence to back up your answer. It is important to start your answer with your opinion, then select pieces of text from the passage to back up your answer, giving an English version of what is in the passage.
- Look closely at each word in each section of the translation passage, and pay particular attention to the articles and tenses used. Make sure you include each word in your translation (although translation is not word for word!). Look at marking schemes for translations to give you an idea of what a good translation should look like.

Directed Writing

- Have a quick look at the two choices for writing, and go for the one for which your prepared material will give you most support.

- Consider, carefully, the wording of each bullet point, and make sure any learned material that you use is relevant and appropriate to the bullet point. Make sure you address each part of the first bullet point, and that you are answering the questions asked.

- Use your dictionary to check the accuracy of what you have written (spelling, genders etc.), but not to create and invent new sentences.

- Don't write pieces that are too long, you only need 120–150 words. So stick to 30–40 words per bullet point.

- Be aware of the extended criteria used in assessing performances in Writing (included in the Answer Section of this book!), so that you know what's required to achieve the good and very good categories in terms of content, accuracy, and range and variety of language.

- Ensure that your handwriting is legible (particularly when writing in Spanish) and distinguish clearly between rough notes and what you wish to be considered as your final answers. Make sure you score out your notes!

- You should bear in mind the following points:

  - There are four bullet points to answer: they are not really predictable and vary from year to year, but certain things come up regularly.

  - Each of the four bullet points should have between 30 and 40 words to address it properly.

  - You will be assessed on how well you have answered the points, and on the accuracy of your language.

  - If you miss out or fail to address a bullet point correctly, the most you can get is six marks.

  - For a mark of good or very good, you should use some complex language such as longer, varied sentences, adjectives and conjunctions.

Listening

- Your listening skills will improve most with practice. So use the Listening sections in this book several times to get used to the format of the exam.

- Read the questions carefully before the first listening and use them as a means of anticipating the sort of information you will need to extract from the text.

- Not giving enough detail is still a major reason for candidates losing marks. Many answers are correct as far as they go, but don't have enough detail to score marks. The same rules as for Reading apply. Give as much detail as possible in your answers and don't lose marks by writing down numbers, prepositions and question words inaccurately.

- You hear each of the two Listening texts twice only, so make use of the gap between the two recordings to check which specific details you still need for your answers, so your listening is focused.

- Make sure you're able to give accurate answers through confident knowledge of numbers, common adjectives, weather expressions, prepositions and question words, so that some of the "easier" points of information are not lost through lack of sufficiently accurate details.

- When responding to the questions in the Listening papers, be guided by the number of points awarded for each question, and by the wording of the question. You should give as much detail in your answer as you have understood, but should not write down everything you hear. The question itself usually indicates the amount of information required by stating in bold, e.g. "Give **2** of them".

- Be sure to put a line through any notes you have made!

Personal Response Writing

- Make sure you read the stimulus questions carefully and adapt any learned material you use so it's relevant to the aspects contained in them.

- There are three questions to be answered, so you should aim for 40/50 words for each of them, however, it is okay to focus on the questions which allow you to write at ease.

- Try to recycle or adapt the material you have already covered on the topic of the essay and you know is accurate, as it might have been marked by your teacher - using and recycling it to tackle the essay.

Good luck!

Remember that the rewards for passing Higher Spanish are well worth it! Your pass will help you get the future you want for yourself. In the exam, be confident in your own ability. If you're not sure how to answer a question, trust your instincts and just give it a go anyway – keep calm and don't panic! GOOD LUCK!

HIGHER

2014 Specimen Question Paper

National
Qualifications
SPECIMEN ONLY

SQ42/H/11

**Spanish
Reading**

Date — Not applicable

Duration — 1 hour and 40 minutes

Total marks — 30

Attempt ALL questions.

Write your answers clearly, in **English**, in the Reading Answer Booklet provided. In the answer booklet you must clearly identify the question number you are attempting.

You may use a Spanish dictionary.

Use **blue** or **black** ink.

There is a separate question and answer booklet for Directed Writing. You must complete your answer for Directed Writing in the question and answer booklet for Directed Writing.

Before leaving the examination room you must give your Reading answer booklet and your Directed Writing question and answer booklet to the Invigilator; if you do not, you may lose all the marks for this paper.

Total marks — 30

This Reading Paper replaces the original one in the SQA Specimen Paper, which cannot be reproduced for copyright reasons. As such, it should be stressed that it is not an official SQA verified section, although every care has been taken by the Publishers to ensure that it offers appropriate practice material for CfE Higher.

Read the whole article carefully and then answer, in English, ALL the questions that follow.

The article discusses the impact of the digital age.

Significado de era digital

¿Qué es la era digital? La era digital, también conocida como era de la información y de las telecomunicaciones es, simplemente, el mundo en el que vivimos actualmente. Esta etapa comenzó cuando se inventó el teléfono, pero la mayor revolución ha sido, sin lugar a dudas, la invención de Internet. La era digital es diferente de las etapas anteriores de
5   la historia, porque ahora la mayoría de la gente puede acceder a cualquier tipo de información de forma muy rápida y barata.

Con la revolución digital podemos hacer casi todo en Internet con un clic del ratón de nuestro ordenador: comprar comida, reservar una habitación de hotel, leer el periódico, ver la televisión, comunicarnos con nuestros amigos... Cada vez existen más y más
10 aplicaciones y programas que hacen nuestra vida más fácil.

También en el trabajo, ha ocurrido toda una revolución. Cada vez en más y más países, el trabajo se hace más fácil y rápido gracias a numerosos programas. Por ejemplo, antes había que escribir un texto a máquina (¡o incluso a mano!), fotocopiarlo y mandarlo por carta o por fax. Sin embargo, ahora se escribe directamente en el ordenador, se pueden
15 incluir gráficos, imágenes, etcétera y luego mandar el documento por correo electrónico. ¡Ahora podemos hacer todo esto incluso utilizando el teléfono móvil! Gracias a esto, los trabajos se van haciendo poco a poco más flexibles y cada vez existen más personas que trabajan desde casa. Sin embargo, no hay que olvidar que no todas las personas tienen acceso a la tecnología de la misma forma. En muchos países del Tercer Mundo, las
20 personas carecen de medios económicos suficientes para comprar un ordenador o un teléfono móvil de última generación, o pagar la cuota de Internet.

Hay muchísimas consecuencias positivas derivadas de las nuevas tecnologías de la comunicación, sin embargo, aquí queremos destacar una: el acceso a la información. En el mundo moderno y gracias a la tecnología, tenemos acceso a todo tipo de información
25 con solo hacer clic en Internet y buscar en un motor de búsqueda como Google. La mayoría de los periódicos y publicaciones se encuentran ya en también en Internet y actualizan la información constantemente. Incluso las noticias que no aparecen en los periódicos, a causa de que no hay espacio suficiente, suelen encontrarse sin problema en Internet, porque allí no hay limitación de espacio físico.

30 Por supuesto, en la era digital no todo es de color de rosa, sino que también encontramos personas que utilizan las nuevas tecnologías para causar daño o sufrimiento, o para comunicar ideas negativas. Por ejemplo, personas que, en su tiempo libre, dejan comentarios en artículos o videos de Internet que atacan personalmente al autor y que solo buscan causar sufrimiento, sin hacer ninguna crítica constructiva.

35 Otro problema que podemos observar es que, en algunos casos, la tecnología nos impide apreciar a las personas y los paisajes que nos rodean, pues estamos más preocupados de ver si tenemos un correo electrónico nuevo o si alguien nos ha dejado un comentario en las redes sociales.

En general, podemos decir que los avances en las tecnologías digitales hacen nuestra vida
40 mucho más fácil, nos conectan con el mundo y con personas que están lejos. Sin embargo, no debemos olvidar prestar atención a las personas que tenemos a nuestro lado.

MARKS

Questions

Re-read lines 1—6

1.	In what way does the article define the digital era?	1
2.	What two inventions started the digital age?	1
3.	What is different about the digital age? Give details.	2

Re-read lines 7—10

4.	In what way do we access data, according to the article?	1
5.	State any three things we can now do, according to the article.	3

Re-read lines 14—21

6.	What have been two effects of the new era?	2
7.	Which people may not have full access to the new era?	1

Re-read lines 24—29

8.	What use do newspapers make of new technologies?	1
9.	What advantage does the internet hold for newspapers?	1

Re-read lines 35—41

10.	What negative effects of the new era does the article note? Give details.	3
11.	What might stop us appreciating the people and places we come across?	2
12.	Now consider the article as a whole. Does the author give positive, negative or balanced view of the impact of new technologies? Justify your answer with reference to the text.	2
13.	Translate into English lines 11—14. (También....fax)	10

[END OF SPECIMEN QUESTION PAPER]

Page three

[BLANK PAGE]

DO NOT WRITE ON THIS PAGE

H

National
Qualifications
SPECIMEN ONLY

Mark

SQ42/H/02

Spanish
Directed Writing

Date — Not applicable

Duration — 1 hour and 40 minutes

Fill in these boxes and read what is printed below.

Full name of centre

Town

Forename(s)

Surname

Number of seat

Date of birth

Day   Month   Year

Scottish candidate number

Total marks — 10

Choose ONE scenario on *Page two* and write your answer clearly, in **Spanish**, in the space provided in this booklet. You must clearly identify the scenario number you are attempting.

You may use a Spanish dictionary.

Additional space for answers is provided at the end of this booklet.

Use **blue** or **black** ink.

There is a separate answer booklet for Reading. You must complete your answers for Reading in the answer booklet for Reading.

Before leaving the examination room you must give this Directed Writing question and answer booklet and your Reading answer booklet to the Invigilator; if you do not, you may lose all the marks for this paper.

Total marks — 10

Choose **one** of the following two scenarios.

SCENARIO 1: Employability

> Last summer, you spent a month working in Spain.
>
> You have been asked to write a report in Spanish for your school/college language webpage about your experience.

You must include the following information and **you should try to add** other relevant details:

- Where you worked **and** how you got the job

- What you had to do every day

- If you got on with your boss and the other employees

- If you would recommend working abroad

You should write approximately 120—150 words.

OR

SCENARIO 2: Culture

> While in Spain/Latin America, you attended a party organised by your Spanish/Latin American friend.
>
> You have been asked to write about your experience in Spanish for the language section of your school/college website.

You must include the following information and **you should try to add** other relevant details:

- Where you went **and** the reason your friend was having a party

- What the people were like that you met at the party

- What you enjoyed most about the party

- What plans you will make if your Spanish friend comes to visit you

You should write approximately 120—150 words.

ANSWER SPACE

MARKS

Scenario number

_____

_____

_____

_____

_____

_____

_____

_____

_____

_____

_____

_____

_____

_____

_____

_____

_____

_____

_____

_____

_____

_____

_____

_____

_____

_____

_____

MARKS | DO NOT WRITE IN THIS MARGIN

ANSWER SPACE (continued)

MARKS | DO NOT WRITE IN THIS MARGIN

ANSWER SPACE (continued)

MARKS | DO NOT WRITE IN THIS MARGIN

ANSWER SPACE (continued)

[END OF SPECIMEN QUESTION PAPER]

ADDITIONAL SPACE FOR ANSWERS

MARKS | DO NOT WRITE IN THIS MARGIN

MARKS | DO NOT WRITE IN THIS MARGIN

ADDITIONAL SPACE FOR ANSWERS

H

National
Qualifications
SPECIMEN ONLY

Mark

SQ42/H/03

Spanish
Listening and Writing

Date — Not applicable

Duration — 1 hour

Fill in these boxes and read what is printed below.

Full name of centre

Town

Forename(s)

Surname

Number of seat

Date of birth

Day	Month	Year

Scottish candidate number

Total marks — 30

SECTION 1 — LISTENING — 20 marks

You will hear two items in Spanish. **Before you hear each item, you will have one minute to study the questions.** You will hear each item twice, with an interval of one minute between playings. You will then have time to answer the questions before hearing the next item. Write your answers clearly, in **English**, in the spaces provided.

SECTION 2 — WRITING — 10 marks

Write your answer clearly, in **Spanish**, in the space provided.

Attempt ALL questions. You may use a Spanish dictionary.

Additional space for answers is provided at the end of this booklet. If you use this space you must clearly identify the question number you are attempting.

You are not allowed to leave the examination room until the end of the test.

Use **blue** or **black** ink.

Before leaving the examination room you must give this booklet to the Invigilator; if you do not, you may lose all the marks for this paper.

MARKS | DO NOT WRITE IN THIS MARGIN

SECTION 1 — LISTENING — 20 marks
Attempt ALL questions

Item 1

You listen to Manuel, who talks about his leisure activities.

(a)   (i)   Why did Manuel stop playing football?   **1**

_____

(ii)   In what ways does he stay involved in football?   Give any **one** detail.   **1**

_____

(b)   Manuel's passion for music started when he was very young.   Give any **one** example.   **1**

_____

(c)   What did Manuel discover in music? Give any **one** detail.   **1**

_____

(d)   Manuel talks about a leisure survey.

(i)   What are the two most common leisure activities amongst Spanish young people?   **2**

_____

_____

(ii)   What surprises Manuel about the results of the survey?   **1**

_____

(e)   Overall, which statement best describes Manuel's feelings about his leisure activities? Tick (✓) the correct statement.   **1**

His leisure activities are identical to those of typical young Spaniards.	
Leisure activities are important to him.	
He hasn't got enough time for his leisure activities.	

MARKS | DO NOT WRITE IN THIS MARGIN

Item 2

You listen to an online interview with a Spanish pop singer, Carmen.

(a) Carmen describes how her professional career started. Give any **two** details about this.

2

_____

_____

(b) Carmen has made the list of "People" magazine's 100 Most Beautiful. What does Carmen think about this? State any **one** thing.

1

_____

(c) Carmen talks about the advantages and disadvantages of being famous.

    (i) State any **one** advantage.

1

_____

    (ii) State any **one** disadvantage.

1

_____

(d) Carmen then talks about what makes her happy.

    (i) What makes Carmen happy?

1

_____

    (ii) She also loves to go back home. Why is this? Give any **one** reason.

1

_____

(e) When does Carmen find inspiration?

1

_____

(f) Apart from sport, what does Carmen do to stay healthy? Give any **two** details.

2

_____

_____

MARKS DO NOT WRITE IN THIS MARGIN

Item 2 (continued)

    (g) Finally, what does Carmen say about languages? Give any **two** details.   2

_____

_____

MARKS | DO NOT WRITE IN THIS MARGIN

SECTION 2 — WRITING — 10 marks

Carmen ha hablado de sus pasatiempos y de lo que hace para mantenerse en forma. Y tú, ¿qué haces para estar en forma? ¿Tienes muchos pasatiempos? ¿Crees que es importante tener pasatiempos sanos?

Escribe 120—150 palabras, en español, para expresar tus ideas.

ANSWER SPACE FOR SECTION 2 (continued)

[END OF SPECIMEN QUESTION PAPER]

ADDITIONAL SPACE FOR ANSWERS

MARKS | DO NOT WRITE IN THIS MARGIN

ADDITIONAL SPACE FOR ANSWERS

National
Qualifications
SPECIMEN ONLY

SQ42/H/13

**Spanish
Listening Transcript**

Date — Not applicable

Duration — 1 hour

This paper must not be seen by any candidate.

The material overleaf is provided for use in an emergency only (eg the recording or equipment proving faulty) or where permission has been given in advance by SQA for the material to be read to candidates with additional support needs. The material must be read exactly as printed.

Transcript — Higher

(t)   Item 1

You listen to Manuel who talks about his leisure activities.

You now have one minute to study the questions for Item 1.

(m) En mi vida tengo dos pasiones, el deporte y la música:

Cuando tenía diez años empecé a jugar al fútbol con mis amigos del barrio. Cada día pasábamos muchas horas juntos en el parque entrenando. Yo era muy buen jugador, y me hubiera gustado ser futbolista profesional. Pero, con doce años empecé a tener problemas con la rodilla y no pude continuar jugando al fútbol, así que dejé de jugar al fútbol. A pesar del problema con la rodilla, para mí, el fútbol sigue siendo importante aunque ahora lo disfruto como espectador. Soy abonado de mi equipo favorito y no me pierdo nunca los partidos. También soy el asistente del entrenador de un equipo de niños pequeños.

Mi pasión por la música me viene desde que era muy joven: por ejemplo, con solo cinco años aprendí a tocar la guitarra, y cuando estaba en la escuela en vez de estudiar escribía canciones. Descubrí que la música era mi forma de expresarme, y una manera de olvidarme de los problemas. Estoy en un grupo de música pop con mis amigos y solemos ensayar casi todos los fines de semana.

La semana pasada leímos una encuesta en el instituto sobre los pasatiempos más populares de los jóvenes españoles: El primero era participar en deportes de equipo, como el fútbol o el baloncesto. El segundo más popular era pasar tiempo hablando con los amigos en las redes sociales. Me sorprende que los jóvenes ahora pasen más tiempo en las redes sociales, chateando con sus amigos en internet, que hablando con sus amigos cara a cara.

(2 minutes)

(t) Item 2

You listen to an online interview with a Spanish pop singer, Carmen.

You now have one minute to study the questions for Item 2.

(m) Hola Carmen, es un placer tenerte aquí con nosotros, muchas gracias.

(f) El placer es mío.

(m) Carmen, ¡te has hecho famosa muy rápidamente!, cuéntanos cómo empezó tu carrera profesional.

(f) Bueno, yo empecé cantando en el sofá blanco de mi casa y puse los videos en las redes sociales. Por esto tengo que reconocer que las nuevas tecnologías han jugado un papel muy importante en mi carrera profesional.

(m) Carmen, según la revista "People" eres una de las cien personas más bellas del mundo. . ., ¿qué piensas sobre esto?

(f) Pues para decir la verdad no me importa en absoluto. Yo me dedico a escribir canciones, a tocar la guitarra, y a lo que más me gusta, a cantar.

(m) Dime Carmen, ¿te gusta ser famosa?

(f) Ser famosa tiene ventajas. Por ejemplo, si me reconocen en un restaurante, insisten que me siente en una de las mejores mesas. Por las calles mucha gente me sonríe o mis fans me piden un autógrafo. Por otro lado, es difícil escaparme, o no llamar la atención. ¡Me gustaría entrar en una tienda sin que los dependientes me reconozcan!

(m) Y ¿qué te hace feliz?

(f) Hay muchas cosas que me hacen feliz, como irme de vacaciones o descansar en la playa pero lo que me encanta es volver a mi casa, a mi tierra, a Málaga, porque echo mucho de menos la comida de mi madre y me gusta pasar tiempo con mi familia.

(m) Cuéntame, ¿cómo buscas la inspiración para tus canciones?

(f) Bueno, como Málaga está en la costa, busco la inspiración cuando doy un paseo por la playa. Además, como estoy muy ocupada, a veces me llega la inspiración incluso hasta en el gimnasio haciendo ejercicio o en clase de zumba.

(m) Ah, en el gimnasio. ¿Y además del deporte, que más haces para mantenerte en forma?

(f) Para mí la salud es muy importante, por ejemplo nunca he fumado. Yo tengo una dieta muy equilibrada, no como mucha grasa e intento dormir ocho horas al día.

(m) Y, para terminar ¿qué tal se te dan los idiomas?

(f) Bueno, hablo francés con fluidez, y en mis conciertos siempre canto una canción en francés Quiero mejorar mi nivel de inglés porque considero que los idiomas son muy importantes. También me gusta escuchar música en inglés.

(2 minutes)

(t) End of test.

Now look over your answers.

[END OF SPECIMEN TRANSCRIPT]

[BLANK PAGE]

DO NOT WRITE ON THIS PAGE

HIGHER

2015

National
Qualifications
2015

X769/76/11

Spanish
Reading

FRIDAY, 29 MAY
9:00 AM – 10:40 AM

Total marks — 30

Attempt ALL questions.

Write your answers clearly, in **English**, in the Reading answer booklet provided. In the answer booklet you must clearly identify the question number you are attempting.

You may use a Spanish dictionary.

Use **blue** or **black** ink.

There is a separate question and answer booklet for Directed Writing. You must complete your answer for Directed Writing in the question and answer booklet for Directed Writing.

Before leaving the examination room you must give your Reading answer booklet and your Directed Writing question and answer booklet to the Invigilator; if you do not, you may lose all the marks for this paper.

Total marks — 30

Attempt ALL questions

Read the whole article carefully and then answer, in **English**, ALL the questions that follow.

You read an article about teenagers and the motivation to study.

La motivación y los adolescentes

Uno de los retos más difíciles para padres y profesores en este momento es cómo motivar a los adolescentes a estudiar. Hay varios factores que suelen contribuir a la falta de motivación en los adolescentes. Pueden perder la motivación cuando pasan de la escuela primaria a la secundaria.

5 En la primaria, los niños trabajan para ser el primero de la clase, para contentar a sus padres, y simplemente porque les fascina aprender cosas nuevas. Pero en el momento de pasar a la escuela secundaria, un adolescente puede sentirse perdido en un nuevo ambiente totalmente distinto o sobrecargado con una mayor cantidad de trabajo escolar.

Según la catedrática Manuela Ricardo Ortiz de la Universidad de Oviedo, las prioridades
10 de los adolescentes, debido a su edad, han cambiado y ahora son otras. "Por ejemplo, ahora sienten la necesidad de ser valorados y de encontrarle sentido a lo que hacen. Quieren tener una pandilla de amigos cercanos y dedicarle mucho tiempo," explica Manuela.

La falta de atención es otro problema que algunos profesores han observado. Dicen que
15 es cada vez más difícil conseguir que los adolescentes se concentren en un proyecto escolar. Esto es porque están acostumbrados a ver programas de televisión breves, y a usar las redes sociales que requieren un bajo nivel de concentración.

El papel de los padres

En primer lugar, es importante enseñar responsabilidad al adolescente. Los padres deben
20 alentar a los adolescentes a comprender que la libertad conlleva responsabilidades. Además, deberían animar a sus hijos a que comprendan que, si quieren tomar decisiones independientes, habrá consecuencias derivadas de sus decisiones.

A Rocío Rodríguez, madre de Isabel y Ana, le parecía muy difícil llegar a motivar a sus hijas adolescentes. "Cuando mis hijas llegaron a la adolescencia, se enfrentaron a tareas
25 más difíciles y se pusieron abrumadas por el trabajo que debían completar; ya no sabían cómo encontrar tiempo para terminar sus tareas. Les ayudé a mis dos hijas a aprender a administrar su tiempo y a elaborar un plan de estudio diario. Siempre les aconsejo que es preferible empezar por lo que menos nos gusta e ir intercalando las asignaturas que nos resultan más complicadas con las que nos resultan más fáciles."

30 ### Expectativas altas en la enseñanza

Según un estudio reciente, las expectativas del profesor tienen un poderoso efecto en el comportamiento y la motivación de los estudiantes. Se trata de que el profesor mantenga expectativas altas de sus estudiantes y que se asegure de que participen activamente en el aula. También, para el profesor, es imprescindible variar los métodos
35 de enseñanza e incrementar progresivamente la dificultad del material de lectura. Esas combinaciones pueden funcionar siempre que, según los estudiantes, se dé un equilibrio realista.

Paco Bernabéu Martínez es profesor de idiomas desde hace veinte años en un instituto en las afueras de Madrid. Reconoce que los profesores tienen un papel importante a la hora
40 de entusiasmar a los adolescentes. "Después de leer el estudio, decidí implementar algunas estrategias para motivar a mis alumnos de cuarto con resultados muy positivos. Algo muy llamativo fue una mejora en el rendimiento escolar. Otra consecuencia importante es que ahora mis alumnos saben desarrollar sus propias habilidades lingüísticas. Esto les da confianza."

Page two

45 **La motivación moral**

Algo que está claro es que los adolescentes necesitan buenas razones para aumentar sus niveles de motivación para estudiar. Según dice Manuela Ricardo Ortiz: "No podemos motivar únicamente a los jóvenes a base de incentivos materiales, esto es, recibiendo recompensas: en general, ya tienen todo lo que quieren y, además, esta idea les genera
50 aburrimiento. A mi modo de ver los jóvenes tienen que darse cuenta de que estudian para aprender a pensar por sí mismos y porque deben formarse para ser útiles a la sociedad. Sólo así serán felices y estarán motivados."

MARKS

Questions

Re-read lines 1—17.

1. The opening of the article states that teenagers can lose motivation when they move from primary to secondary school.

    (a) What motivates children to work in class at primary school? State any **two** things.   2

    (b) How do teenagers sometimes feel when they move to secondary school? Give details of any **one** thing.   1

2. According to Manuela Ricardo Ortiz, in what ways have the priorities of teenagers changed? State any **two** things.   2

Re-read lines 18—29.

3. The article discusses the role of parents.

    What should they encourage their teenagers to do? Give details.   2

4. Rocío Rodríguez is a mother of two teenage daughters.

    (a) What happened to her daughters when they became teenagers? State any **two** things.   2

    (b) Rocío helped them to manage their time. What does she always advise them to do? Give details.   2

Re-read lines 30—52

5. According to a recent study, in what ways can teachers also help to motivate their students? State any **three** things.   3

MARKS

6. Paco Bernabéu Martínez implemented some of the strategies of the study. What positive results did he see? State any **two** things.

2

7. According to Manuela Ricardo Ortiz, young people cannot be motivated only by receiving rewards.

   (a) Why is this? Give any **one** reason.

1

   (b) What must young people realise? State any **one** thing.

1

8. Now consider the article as a whole. What is the writer's opinion on strategies to motivate teenagers to study? Justify your answer with reference to the text.

2

9. Translate into English the underlined section:

   "La falta . . . concentración." (lines 14–17)

10

[END OF QUESTION PAPER]

H National Qualifications 2015

Mark

X769/76/02

Spanish Directed Writing

FRIDAY, 29 MAY

9:00 AM – 10:40 AM

Fill in these boxes and read what is printed below.

Full name of centre

Town

Forename(s)

Surname

Number of seat

Date of birth

Day   Month   Year   Scottish candidate number

Total marks — 10

Choose ONE scenario on *Page two* and write your answer clearly, in **Spanish**, in the space provided in this booklet. You must clearly identify the scenario number you are attempting.

You may use a Spanish dictionary.

Additional space for answers is provided at the end of this booklet.

Use **blue** or **black** ink.

There is a separate answer booklet for Reading. You must complete your answers for Reading in the answer booklet for Reading.

Before leaving the examination room you must give this Directed Writing question and answer booklet and your Reading answer booklet to the Invigilator; if you do not, you may lose all the marks for this paper.

Total marks — 10

Choose **one** of the following two scenarios.

SCENARIO 1: Culture

> While in Spain, you took part in a local festival. You have been asked to write about your experience in Spanish for the language section of your school/ college website.

You must include the following information and **you should try to add** other relevant details:

- How you travelled **and** what the journey was like
- What you enjoyed most about the festival
- What else you did during your stay in Spain
- If you would recommend such an experience to others

You should write approximately 120–150 words.

OR

SCENARIO 2: Society

> Last year you took part in a language exchange in Spain where you stayed with a Spanish family. You have been asked to write about your experience in Spanish for the language section of your school/college website.

You must include the following information and **you should try to add** other relevant details:

- How you travelled **and** what you thought of the journey
- How you helped around the house
- What you did to improve your Spanish
- If you would recommend an experience like this to other young people

You should write approximately 120–150 words.

ANSWER SPACE

Scenario number

ANSWER SPACE (continued)

ANSWER SPACE (continued)

MARKS | DO NOT WRITE IN THIS MARGIN

ANSWER SPACE (continued)

[END OF QUESTION PAPER]

ADDITIONAL SPACE FOR ANSWERS

MARKS | DO NOT WRITE IN THIS MARGIN

MARKS | DO NOT WRITE IN THIS MARGIN

ADDITIONAL SPACE FOR ANSWERS

H

National Qualifications 2015

Mark

X769/76/03

**Spanish
Listening and Writing**

FRIDAY, 29 MAY

11:30 AM – 12:30 PM

Fill in these boxes and read what is printed below.

Full name of centre

Town

Forename(s)

Surname

Number of seat

Date of birth

Day   Month   Year   Scottish candidate number

Total marks — 30

SECTION 1 — LISTENING — 20 marks.

You will hear two items in Spanish. **Before you hear each item, you will have one minute to study the question.** You will hear each item twice, with an interval of one minute between playings. You will then have time to answer the questions before hearing the next item. Write your answers clearly, in **English**, in the spaces provided.

SECTION 2 — WRITING — 10 marks.

Write your answer clearly, in **Spanish**, in the space provided.

Attempt ALL questions. You may use a Spanish dictionary.

Additional space for answers is provided at the end of this booklet. If you use this space you must clearly identify the question number you are attempting.

You are not allowed to leave the examination room until the end of the test.

Use **blue** or **black** ink.

Before leaving the examination room you must give this booklet to the Invigilator; if you do not, you may lose all the marks for this paper.

MARKS | DO NOT WRITE IN THIS MARGIN

SECTION 1 — LISTENING — 20 marks

Attempt ALL questions

Item 1

Ana talks about her future career.

(a) Ana would like to be an engineer. Why is this? Give any **one** reason.   **1**

_____

(b)   (i) How does she describe the university in her city?   **1**

_____

(ii) Why does she want to move to another city? Give any **one** reason.   **1**

_____

(iii) What do her parents recognise she must do? Give any **one** detail.   **1**

_____

(c) Ana describes the skills you need to be an engineer. Which skills are important? State any **two**.   **2**

_____

_____

(d) Why will Ana also learn a language at university? Give any **one** reason.   **1**

_____

(e) Overall, which statement best describes Ana's suitability for her chosen career? Tick (✓) the correct statement.   **1**

	Tick (✓)
She is confident about her skills.	
She has some doubt about her skills.	
She will need to travel abroad to get experience.	

MARKS | DO NOT WRITE IN THIS MARGIN

Item 2

Guillermo López takes part in an interview about his job as a television actor.

(a) Guillermo talks about how his acting career started. Give any **two** details about this.

2

_____

_____

(b) He found his first job in television.

(i) What was surprising about this job?

1

_____

(ii) In what way did it help him to become a better actor?

1

_____

(c) Guillermo talks about his daily routine in the job he does now. What does he do before starting to film scenes? Give **two** details.

2

_____

_____

(d) He describes a normal day when he is **not** working. What does he do? Give any **two** details.

2

_____

_____

(e) What would Guillermo like to do in the future? Give any **two** details.

2

_____

_____

(f) According to Guillermo, there will always be work in the television industry. Why is this? Give any **two** details.

2

_____

_____

SECTION 2 — WRITING — 10 marks

Ana ha hablado de su carrera profesional y de sus destrezas. ¿Qué tipo de proyectos te gustaría hacer en el futuro? ¿Te gustaría seguir estudiando? ¿Cuáles son tus destrezas y habilidades?

Escribe 120–150 palabras, en español, para expresar tus ideas.

MARKS | DO NOT WRITE IN THIS MARGIN

ANSWER SPACE FOR SECTION 2 (continued)

MARKS | DO NOT WRITE IN THIS MARGIN

ANSWER SPACE FOR SECTION 2 (continued)

[END OF QUESTION PAPER]

ADDITIONAL SPACE FOR ANSWERS

MARKS | DO NOT WRITE IN THIS MARGIN

ADDITIONAL SPACE FOR ANSWERS

National
Qualifications
2015

X769/76/13

Spanish
Listening Transcript

FRIDAY, 29 MAY
11:30 AM – 12:30 PM

This paper must not be seen by any candidate.

The material overleaf is provided for use in an emergency only (eg the recording or equipment proving faulty) or where permission has been given in advance by SQA for the material to be read to candidates with additional support needs. The material must be read exactly as printed.

Instructions to reader(s):

For each item, read the English **once**, then read the Spanish **twice**, with an interval of 1 minute between the two readings. On completion of the second reading, pause for the length of time indicated in brackets after the item, to allow the candidates to write their answers.

Where special arrangements have been agreed in advance to allow the reading of the material, those sections marked **(f)** should be read by a female speaker and those marked **(m)** by a male; those sections marked **(t)** should be read by the teacher.

(t) Item Number One

Ana talks about her future career.

You now have one minute to study the questions for Item Number One.

(f) Debo admitir que desde pequeña tengo muy clara mi vocación—ser ingeniera. Siempre me han interesado las ciencias y las matemáticas en el instituto y además, me interesa ver cómo funcionan las cosas. Sé que en el futuro quiero trabajar usando mis conocimientos científicos. Por esto he decidido estudiar ingeniería en la universidad, y creo que tengo la motivación suficiente para alcanzar mis sueños.

En mi ciudad, hay una universidad con fama internacional y he considerado estudiar aquí. Pero al final he decidido que a mí me gustaría mudarme a otra ciudad, porque me apetece alquilar un piso con mis mejores amigos, y estar lejos de mis padres ¡será fenomenal! Mis padres prefieren que me quede con ellos. Sin embargo, reconocen que debo aprender a independizarme y a vivir por mi cuenta. Y claro, tienen razón.

En mi opinión, ser ingeniera significa que tengo que ser una persona con muchas habilidades importantes. Y ¿cuáles son? Pues, por ejemplo, hay que ser trabajador, poder colaborar en equipo y también demostrar capacidades de liderazgo. Yo creo que tengo las habilidades necesarias, y seguro que voy a desarrollar más destrezas cuando esté estudiando.

En el futuro, en la universidad, aprenderé otro idioma ya que existen muchas ofertas de trabajo en otros países. Me encantaría pasar un año viviendo en el extranjero.

(2 minutes)

(t) **Item Number Two**

Guillermo López takes part in an interview about his job as a television actor.

You now have one minute to study the questions for Item Number Two.

(f) Hola Guillermo, ¿qué tal?

(m) Pues en este momento estoy bien.

(f) Guillermo, has trabajado en una serie de televisión que tiene mucho éxito. ¿Me puedes explicar cómo empezaste tu carrera?

(m) Por supuesto. De niño siempre me interesaba el teatro y era miembro de un club de cine en el colegio. Decidí estudiar arte dramático en la universidad y después conseguí trabajo en la tele. ¡Qué suerte tuve!

(f) Ah, ¿tu primer trabajo fue en la tele?

(m) Sí, y lo más sorprendente es que trabajaba detrás de las cámaras. Pero me gustaba mucho, y me ayudaba a mejorar como actor porque podía aprender mucho de los otros actores.

(f) Um y, ¿qué haces ahora?

(m) Ahora ya no trabajo detrás de las cámaras. Soy actor en una telenovela muy famosa.

(f) ¿Me puedes hablar de un día típico de trabajo?

(m) Pues sí claro. Normalmente llego al estudio a las ocho de la mañana para empezar a las ocho y media. Antes de rodar las escenas, siempre tomamos el desayuno en equipo. ¡Qué hambre! También me pongo a leer los mensajes que me envían mis fans. A la hora de comer leo noticias de mi familia y mis amigos en las redes sociales y memorizo los guiones.

(f) Y cuando no trabajas, ¿cómo es un día normal en tu vida?

(m) Bueno, aprovecho el tiempo libre para pasar tiempo con mi mujer y con mi hijo. También, suelo salir a comer con amigos por el casco antiguo de la ciudad. Otras veces salgo a dar un paseo por la playa. Soy afortunado porque solamente trabajo cuatro días a la semana.

(f) Ah, ¿qué tipo de proyectos te gustaría hacer en el futuro?

(m) Llevo un tiempo pensando mucho en el futuro. Creo que me gustaría centrarme más en proyectos cinematográficos, pero sobre todo trabajar en historias que tengan un mensaje social. También me ilusionaría viajar por el mundo con mi familia.

(f) Y finalmente, ¿hay mucho trabajo en la televisión?

(m) Sí, hay mucho trabajo y siempre habrá trabajo en esta industria porque yo creo que la gente siempre quiere ver algo en la televisión, quizás para escaparse de su realidad por un momento. Otros ven la televisión para informarse o porque tienen ganas de reírse y por eso tenemos que continuar produciendo programas y series.

(t) **End of Recording.**

[END OF TRANSCRIPT]

Page four

[BLANK PAGE]

DO NOT WRITE ON THIS PAGE

HIGHER

2016

National
Qualifications
2016

X769/76/11

Spanish
Reading

THURSDAY, 26 MAY
9:00 AM – 10:40 AM

Total marks — 30

Attempt ALL questions.

Write your answers clearly, in **English**, in the Reading answer booklet provided. In the answer booklet you must clearly identify the question number you are attempting.

You may use a Spanish dictionary.

Use **blue** or **black** ink.

There is a separate question and answer booklet for Directed Writing. You must complete your answer for Directed Writing in the question and answer booklet for Directed Writing.

Before leaving the examination room you must give your Reading answer booklet and your Directed Writing question and answer booklet to the Invigilator; if you do not, you may lose all the marks for this paper.

Total marks — 30

Attempt ALL questions

Read the whole article carefully and then answer, in **English**, ALL the questions that follow.

You read an article about reducing food waste.

Aquí no se tira nada

De una comida pueden sacarse cinco. La cocina tradicional ha vuelto a muchos hogares españoles por la falta de recursos económicos y por el deseo de ser más creativos con los ingredientes. Según los resultados de un estudio reciente de la Confederación Española de Consumidores, no es sorprendente descubrir que el 86% de los alimentos que se tiran son
5   sobras de otras comidas. Sin embargo otros estudios muestran que las costumbres de los consumidores se han modificado: los consumidores han reducido la cantidad de alimentos que va a la basura y reutilizan con más frecuencia productos como el aceite.

Planear con antelación

La planificación antes de ir al súper es una de las bases para ahorrar en la cesta de la
10   compra. En España se desperdician alrededor de 3 millones de toneladas de alimentos cada año. Un hogar medio tira mucha comida cada año, y casi la mitad de estos alimentos tirados podría haberse consumido si la gente hubiera comprado solo lo necesario.

Jaime Pérez vive con su mujer y sus dos niños en Tarragona. Como muchas familias españolas, gastaban cada vez más en el supermercado. Jaime nos cuenta: "Mi mujer y yo
15   decidimos seguir unas reglas para intentar reducir la cantidad de comida que tiramos mensualmente y también para ahorrar algo de dinero para los gastos de los niños." Jaime explica las reglas que siguen sin dificultades. En familia, planifican semanalmente el menú. Además, tienen en cuenta quién va a estar en casa cada tarde y solo cocinan lo suficiente para ellos. Finalmente, congelan la comida sobrante para usarla en los días siguientes. "Se
20   nota la diferencia tanto en el bolsillo como en la basura" dice Jaime.

Otra solución que podría reducir el desperdicio es compartir una comida casera alrededor de la mesa. Por desgracia, debido al ritmo de trabajo, reuniones y demás compromisos diarios, comer en casa con la familia o los amigos se limita normalmente a los fines de semana. Para los demás días, existe la opción de salir a cenar a un restaurante cercano.

25   ### Talleres de cocina

Por toda España, hay talleres que enseñan a cocinar, como el del *Centro de Cocina Internacional* en Madrid. El objetivo de las personas que asisten es aprender a cocinar con creatividad. Al último taller que realizaron, asistieron doce personas que cocinaron un plato internacional diferente para cada día de la semana. Cada persona creó una serie
30   de recetas, asegurándose de que la alimentación fuese sana, equilibrada y con pocas calorías.

Antonio Madroño, uno de los asistentes al taller explica: "Lo más útil que he aprendido es que se debería seguir un menú para la semana entera y que se puede ser creativo utilizando las sobras como se hacía antes. Para la mayoría de los hogares españoles, hoy en día el
35   desafío es combinar las tradiciones culinarias con las demandas de la vida moderna".

La aplicación *Supercomida*

La tecnología también puede ayudar a hacer una compra más económica. Hay una aplicación llamada *Supercomida* que te permite comparar precios en los supermercados más cercanos y conseguir un ahorro de hasta el 40%: simplemente hay que escanear el código de
40   barras del producto. Otra ventaja de *Supercomida* es que, si pones los ingredientes que te quedan en la nevera, la aplicación sugiere una gama de posibles platos.

Es evidente que en España se está haciendo un gran esfuerzo para reducir la cantidad de comida que se tira: sin duda, esto tendrá beneficios económicos y sociales. Como dice Jaime Pérez, "la basura en nuestra casa está más vacía y tenemos el bolsillo más lleno".

Page two

MARKS

Questions

Re-read lines 1–7.

1. The article states that traditional cooking has returned to many Spanish homes. Why is this?   **2**

2. The results of a recent study provide statistics about food waste.

   (a) What is the significance of 86%?   **1**

   (b) What do other studies show about consumers? Give details.   **3**

Re-read lines 8–24.

3. What does the article say about almost half of the food Spanish people throw away? Give details.   **1**

4. Jaime Pérez and his family follow some rules for shopping.

   (a) These rules help to reduce food waste. What else do the rules help him and his wife to do?   **1**

   (b) Apart from planning their weekly menu, which **three** rules do they follow?   **3**

Re-read lines 25–35.

5. The article gives information about cookery classes.

   (a) Why do people attend these classes?   **1**

   (b) What did the 12 people at the last cookery class do? State **two** things.   **2**

   (c) Antonio Madroño, who went to one of the cookery classes, describes the challenge facing Spanish households. What is this challenge?   **1**

Re-read lines 36–44.

6. What does the App "*Supercomida*" enable shoppers to do? Give **three** details.   **3**

7. Now consider the article as a whole. In the writer's opinion how easy is it to reduce food waste? Justify your answer with reference to the text.   **2**

MARKS

8. Translate into English:

   "Otra solución . . . restaurante cercano" (lines 21—24).   10

[END OF QUESTION PAPER]

H

National
Qualifications
2016

Mark

X769/76/02

**Spanish
Directed Writing**

THURSDAY, 26 MAY

9:00 AM — 10:40 AM

Fill in these boxes and read what is printed below.

Full name of centre

Town

Forename(s)

Surname

Number of seat

Date of birth

Day	Month	Year	Scottish candidate number

Total marks — 10

Choose ONE scenario on *Page two* and write your answer clearly, in **Spanish**, in the space provided in this booklet. You must clearly identify the scenario number you are attempting.

You may use a Spanish dictionary.

Additional space for answers is provided at the end of this booklet.

Use **blue** or **black** ink.

There is a separate answer booklet for Reading. You must complete your answers for Reading in the answer booklet for Reading.

Before leaving the examination room you must give this Directed Writing question and answer booklet and your Reading answer booklet to the Invigilator; if you do not, you may lose all the marks for this paper.

MARKS | DO NOT WRITE IN THIS MARGIN

Total marks — 10

Choose **one** from the following two scenarios.

Scenario 1: Employability

> Last year you worked in a hotel in Spain. You have been asked to write about your experience in Spanish for the language section of your school/college website.

You must include the following information and **you should try to add** other relevant details:

- What the hotel was like **and** what you thought of the facilities
- What your daily routine was
- What skills you had to use in your job
- If you would recommend working abroad to your friends

You should write approximately 120–150 words.

OR

Scenario 2: Culture

> You went to a music festival in a Spanish town with your Spanish class. You have been asked to write about your experience in Spanish for the language section of your school/college website.

You must include the following information and **you should try to add** other relevant details:

- Where you went **and** what you thought of the town
- What you did during the music festival
- How you used your knowledge of Spanish
- If you would like to attend a similar event in the future

You should write approximately 120–150 words.

ANSWER SPACE

Scenario number

MARKS | DO NOT WRITE IN THIS MARGIN

ANSWER SPACE (continued)

ANSWER SPACE (continued)

MARKS | DO NOT WRITE IN THIS MARGIN

ANSWER SPACE (continued)

[END OF QUESTION PAPER]

ADDITIONAL SPACE FOR ANSWERS

MARKS DO NOT WRITE IN THIS MARGIN

ADDITIONAL SPACE FOR ANSWERS

H

National Qualifications 2016

Mark

X769/76/03

**Spanish
Listening and Writing**

THURSDAY, 26 MAY

11:30 AM – 12:30 PM

Fill in these boxes and read what is printed below.

Full name of centre

Town

Forename(s)

Surname

Number of seat

Date of birth

Day	Month	Year	Scottish candidate number

Total marks — 30

SECTION 1 — LISTENING — 20 marks.

You will hear two items in Spanish. **Before you hear each item, you will have one minute to study the question.** You will hear each item twice, with an interval of one minute between playings. You will then have time to answer the questions before hearing the next item. Write your answers clearly, in **English**, in the spaces provided.

SECTION 2 — WRITING — 10 marks.

Write your answer clearly, in **Spanish**, in the space provided.

Attempt ALL questions. You may use a Spanish dictionary.

Additional space for answers is provided at the end of this booklet. If you use this space you must clearly identify the question number you are attempting.

You are not allowed to leave the examination room until the end of the test.

Use **blue** or **black** ink.

Before leaving the examination room you must give this booklet to the Invigilator; if you do not, you may lose all the marks for this paper.

MARKS | DO NOT WRITE IN THIS MARGIN

SECTION 1 — LISTENING — 20 marks

Attempt ALL questions

Item 1

Javi talks about a school trip to Scotland.

(a) How long did Javi spend at the summer camp in the north of Scotland?   1

_____

(b) Javi developed a number of skills at the camp. State any **two**.   2

_____

(c) The group climbed a mountain. Why did Javi like this? Give any **one** reason.   1

_____

(d) Javi also took part in water sports. Why did he not like them?   1

_____

(e) The group had English classes each evening after dinner. What surprising thing did Javi learn?   1

_____

(f) What has Javi decided to do as a result of this experience?   1

_____

(g) Overall, which statement best describes Javi's attitude to his school trip? Tick (✓) the correct statement.   1

	Tick (✓)
He would like to do the same thing next year.	
He has benefitted from the trip.	
He enjoyed all aspects of the trip.	

MARKS | DO NOT WRITE IN THIS MARGIN

Item 2

Pablo asks Carmen about her final year at high school.

(a) Carmen studies economics and two languages at school. Why did she choose to study these subjects? Give **two** reasons.

    2

_____

_____

(b) What is her school like? Give any **three** details.

    3

_____

_____

_____

(c) What does Carmen do in her language classes? Give any **two** details.

    2

_____

_____

(d) Carmen talks about the teachers in her school.

  (i) What do the younger pupils say about the teachers? Give any **two** details.

    2

_____

_____

  (ii) What difference does she notice now that she is older? Give any **two** details.

    2

_____

_____

(e) Carmen intends to study economics at university. What would she like to do after this?

    1

_____

_____

[Turn over

MARKS | DO NOT WRITE IN THIS MARGIN

SECTION 2 — WRITING — 10 marks

Carmen ha hablado de su escuela y de sus estudios. ¿Qué estudias este curso en el instituto? ¿Por qué crees que es importante estudiar idiomas? ¿Qué planes tienes para el futuro?

Escribe 120–150 palabras, en español, para expresar tus ideas.

MARKS | DO NOT WRITE IN THIS MARGIN

ANSWER SPACE FOR SECTION 2 (continued)

[Turn over

MARKS | DO NOT WRITE IN THIS MARGIN

ANSWER SPACE FOR SECTION 2 (continued)

[END OF QUESTION PAPER]

MARKS | DO NOT WRITE IN THIS MARGIN

ADDITIONAL SPACE FOR ANSWERS

MARKS | DO NOT WRITE IN THIS MARGIN

ADDITIONAL SPACE FOR ANSWERS

National Qualifications 2016

X769/76/13

Spanish Listening Transcript

THURSDAY, 26 MAY

11:30 AM – 12:30 PM

This paper must not be seen by any candidate.

The material overleaf is provided for use in an emergency only (eg the recording or equipment proving faulty) or where permission has been given in advance by SQA for the material to be read to candidates with additional support needs. The material must be read exactly as printed.

Instructions to reader(s):

For each item, read the English **once**, then read the Spanish **twice**, with an interval of 1 minute between the two readings. On completion of the second reading of Item Number One, pause for the length of time indicated in brackets after the item, to allow the candidates to write their answers.

Where special arrangements have been agreed in advance to allow the reading of the material, those sections marked **(f)** should be read by a female speaker and those marked **(m)** by a male; those sections marked **(t)** should be read by the teacher.

(t)   Item Number One

Javi talks about a school trip to Scotland.

You now have one minute to study the questions for Item Number One.

(m/f) Acabo de volver de Escocia donde pasé seis semanas en un campamento de verano en el norte de Escocia. Fue un viaje escolar organizado por mi profesor de inglés y éramos un grupo de doce alumnos.

Al principio, estaba un poco inseguro pero poco a poco empecé a relajarme y divertirme porque me lo pasé bomba con la gente que conocí.

En el campamento hicimos una serie de actividades con el objetivo de desarrollar las habilidades de liderazgo, las capacidades de comunicación y del trabajo en equipo.

Una de las actividades fue escalar una montaña en grupo. Disfruté de esta experiencia porque me encanta la naturaleza y pasar tiempo al aire libre. Otro factor positivo fue que nos apoyamos los unos a los otros. Un día, fuimos a un lago donde nos enseñaron a hacer deportes acuáticos. No me gustaron porque no pude soportar el frío del agua dado que estoy acostumbrado al clima mediterráneo.

Por la tarde, después de cenar, asistimos a clases de inglés. Me sorprendió mucho aprender que existen tantas expresiones y palabras que sólo se usan en Escocia.

Como consecuencia de mi experiencia, he decidido solicitar un puesto de instructor en un campamento de verano aquí en España.

(2 minutes)

(t)   **Item Number Two**

Pablo asks Carmen about her final year at high school.

You now have one minute to study the questions for Item Number Two.

(m)   Hola Carmen. ¿Qué tal?

(f)   Pues muy cansada, he pasado toda la noche haciendo deberes.

(m)   Ah sí, ¿Y qué es lo que estás estudiando este año?

(f)   Hago un curso de económicas con idiomas. Creo que he aprendido muchísimo estudiando dos idiomas. Elegí estudiar estas tres asignaturas porque se me dan bien las matemáticas y quiero saber más sobre culturas muy distintas.

(m)   ¡Qué bien! A mí también me gustan las mates. Y Carmen, dime ¿Cómo es tu instituto?

(f)   Pues, mi instituto está recién construido y es muy espacioso. Está en las afueras de la ciudad donde yo vivo. Hay una planta entera dedicada a la tecnología y tiene campos de deporte fenomenales y un gimnasio bien equipado y súper moderno. Tiene muy buena fama con respecto al deporte.

(m)   ¿Y qué tipo de actividades haces en las clases de idiomas?

(f)   Bueno, un montón de cosas. Hacemos muchas actividades interactivas, utilizando la pizarra digital. Puede ser divertido. Lo que más me gusta es cuando hacemos ejercicios de gramática en clase. También leemos revistas sobre la actualidad en otros países.

(m)   ¿Y tus profesores, te llevas bien con ellos?

(f)   Pues sí, pero es normal en el último curso, ¿no? Como ya sabes los alumnos más jóvenes dicen que los profesores son muy estrictos y encima se quejan de que no les dejan hablar mucho en clase, pero reconocen que el profesorado es justo. Pero ahora es diferente. Yo noto mucho la diferencia. Los profesores exigen mucho en cuanto a la calidad de trabajo a pesar de tener un ambiente más relajado. Es verdad que nos dan mucha más responsabilidad.

(m)   Todo el mundo dice eso, que es más relajado en el último curso. ¿Y has pensado en lo que vas a hacer después de terminar el instituto?

(f)   Bueno, como imaginas mi intención después del instituto es ir a la universidad para estudiar económicas. Cuando termine mi carrera universitaria espero montar mi propio negocio.

(m)   Pues, me suena genial.

(f)   Sí Pablo, pero ahora tengo que volver con los deberes.

(t)   **End of recording.**

[END OF TRANSCRIPT]

Page four

[BLANK PAGE]

DO NOT WRITE ON THIS PAGE

HIGHER

Answers

SQA HIGHER
SPANISH 2016

HIGHER SPANISH
2014 SPECIMEN QUESTION PAPER

Reading (replacement Paper)

Question		Expected Answer(s)	Max mark
1		The world we live in now	1
2		The telephone and the internet	1
3		• Most people can access all kinds of information • Quickly and cheaply	2
4		With the click of a mouse on our computer	1
5		Buy food, book a hotel room, read a newspaper, watch tv, communicate with our friends *(any three)*	3
6		• Work is becoming more flexible • More and more people are working from home	2
7		People in the third world	1
8		They update the news constantly	1
9		There are no limitations of space/they can include more news	1
10		• Some people use the internet to cause harm • They communicate negative ideas • Leave negative comments on articles or videos which attack the author • They only want to cause suffering/are never constructive *(any three)*	3
11		• Always checking if we have a new email • Seeing if someone has left us a message on social media	2

Question		Expected Answer(s)	Max mark
12		Award 1 mark for making an assertion and 1 mark for making at least one justification. It can be done in a number of ways: e.g. The writer thinks the digital age has had a positive impact/negative impact. Alternatively, candidates could also say: The writer thinks the digital age has had both a positive and a negative impact as he points out positive and negative aspects giving a balanced picture. The assertion is awarded 1 mark. The justifications given to the assertion should not contradict the gist of the text nor the candidate's assertion. Examples of justifications could include: • He mentions things we can do • Apps and programmes make our life easier • Work is easier and faster • Poor people in the Third World are disadvantaged • Some people abuse the internet If the candidate uses Spanish text uplifted from the passage, it needs to be translated into English and the candidate needs to justify how that text justifies her/his assertion.	2
13		At work a revolution has also taken place/every day in more and more countries/work is getting easier and faster due to numerous programmes/ for example, previously you had to write a text on a typewriter (or even by hand)/ photocopy it and send it by letter or fax	2

Directed Writing

Candidates will write a piece of extended writing in Spanish addressing a scenario that has four related bullet points. Candidates must address each bullet point. The first bullet point contains two pieces of information to be addressed. The remaining three bullet points contain one piece of information each. There is a choice of two scenarios and learners must choose one of these.

Mark	Content	Accuracy	Language resource: variety, range, structures
10	• The content is comprehensive • All bullet points are addressed fully and some candidates may also provide additional relevant information	• The language is accurate in all four bullets. However, where the candidate attempts to go beyond the range of the task, a slightly higher number of inaccuracies need not detract from the overall very good impression • A comprehensive range of verbs is used accurately and tenses are consistent and accurate • There is evidence of confident handling of all aspects of grammar and accurate spelling, although the language may contain a number of minor errors, or even one serious error • Where the candidate attempts to go beyond the range of the task, a slightly higher number of inaccuracies need not detract from the overall very good impression	• The language used is detailed and complex • There is good use of adjectives, adverbs, prepositional phrases and, where appropriate, word order • A comprehensive range of verbs/verb forms, tenses and constructions is used • Some modal verbs and infinitives may be used • The candidate is comfortable with the first person of the verb and generally uses a different verb in each sentence • Sentences are mainly complex and accurate • The language flows well
8	• The content is clear • All bullet points are addressed clearly. The response to one bullet point may be thin, although other bullet points are dealt with in some detail	• The language is mostly accurate. Where the candidate attempts to use detailed and complex language, this may be less successful, although basic structures are used accurately • A range of verbs is used accurately and tenses are generally consistent and accurate • There may be a few errors in spelling, adjective endings and, where relevant, case endings. Use of accents is less secure, where relevant	• The language used is detailed and complex • In one bullet point the language may be more basic than might otherwise be expected at this level • The candidate uses a range of verbs/verb forms and other constructions • There may be less variety in the verbs used • The candidate is comfortable with the first person of the verb and generally uses a different verb in each sentence • Sentences are generally complex and mainly accurate • Overall the writing will be very competent, essentially correct, but may be pedestrian

Mark	Content	Accuracy	Language resource: variety, range, structures
6	• The content is adequate and may be similar to that of an 8 • Bullet points may be addressed adequately, however one of the bullet points may not be addressed	• The language may be mostly accurate in two or three bullet points. However, in the remaining one or two, control of the language structure may deteriorate significantly • The verbs are generally correct, but basic • Tenses may be inconsistent, with present tenses being used at times instead of past tenses • There may be errors in spelling, adjective endings and some prepositions may be inaccurate or omitted. There are quite a few errors in other parts of speech — personal pronouns, gender of nouns, adjective endings, cases (where relevant), singular/plural confusion — and in the use of accents (where relevant) • Overall, there is more correct than incorrect and there is the impression that the candidate can handle tenses	• There are some examples of detailed and complex language • The language is perhaps repetitive and uses a limited range of verbs and fixed phrases not appropriate to this level • The candidate relies on a limited range of vocabulary and structures • There is minimal use of adjectives, probably mainly after "is" • The candidate has a limited knowledge of plurals • A limited range of verbs is used to address some of the bullet points • The candidate copes with the past tense of some verbs • When using the perfect tense, the past participle is incorrect or the auxiliary verb is omitted on occasion • Sentences are mainly single clause and may be brief
4	• The content may be limited and the Directed Writing may be presented as a single paragraph • Bullet points may be addressed in a limited way or • **Two** of the bullet points are not be addressed	• The language is mainly inaccurate and after the first bullet the control of the language structure may deteriorate significantly • A limited range of verbs is used • Ability to form tenses is inconsistent • In the use of the perfect tense the auxiliary verb is omitted on a number of occasions • There may be confusion between the singular and plural form of verbs • There are errors in many other parts of speech — gender of nouns, cases, singular/plural confusion — and in spelling and, where appropriate, word order • Several errors are serious, perhaps showing mother tongue interference	• There is limited use of detailed and complex language • The language is repetitive, with undue reliance on fixed phrases and a limited range of common basic verbs such as to be, to have, to play, to watch • The candidate mainly copes only with simple language • The verbs "was" and "went" may also be used correctly • Sentences are basic and there may be one sentence that is not intelligible to a sympathetic native speaker • An English word may appear in the writing or a word may be omitted • There may be an example of serious dictionary misuse
2	• The content may be basic or similar to that of a 4 or even a 6 • Bullet points are addressed with difficulty	• The language is inaccurate in all four bullets and there is little control of language structure • Many of the verbs are incorrect or even omitted. There is little evidence of tense control • There are many errors in other parts of speech — personal pronouns, gender of nouns, cases, singular/plural confusion, prepositions, for instance	• There is little use, if any, of detailed and complex language • Verbs used more than once may be written differently on each occasion • The candidate displays almost no knowledge of the past tense of verbs • The candidate cannot cope with more than one or two basic verbs • Sentences are very short and some sentences may not be understood by a sympathetic native speaker

Mark	Content	Accuracy	Language resource: variety, range, structures
0	• The content is very basic • The candidate is unable to address the bullet points Or • **Three** or more of the bullet points are not be addressed	• The language is seriously inaccurate in all four bullets and there is almost no control of language structure • Most errors are serious • Virtually nothing is correct • Very little is intelligible to a sympathetic native speaker	• There is no evidence of detailed and complex language • The candidate may only cope with the verbs to have and to be • There may be several examples of mother tongue interference • English words are used • Very few words are written correctly in the modern language. • There may be several examples of serious dictionary misuse

Section 1 — Listening

Item 1

Question			Expected Answer(s)
1	a	i	• He had problems with his knee
1	a	ii	• He has a season ticket/is a supporter of his favourite team • He never misses his favourite team's games/matches • He is an assistant coach for a team of small children *Any one of the above 3 points for 1 mark*
1	b		• At five he played the guitar • At school he wrote songs
1	c		• A form of expressing himself • A way of forgetting his problems *Any one of the above 2 points for 1 mark*
1	d	i	• (To participate in) team sports • (To participate in) social networks
1	d	ii	• Young people spend more time communicating via social networks than face to face
1	e		• Leisure activities are really important to him

Item 2

Question		Expected Answer(s)
2	a	• She started singing on her (white) sofa at home • Posting her videos on social networks • New technologies were very important *Any two of the above 3 points for 2 marks*
2	b	• She doesn't care/it does not matter/she doesn't care at all • Her job is to sing/play the guitar/write songs *Any one of the above 2 points for 1 mark*
2	c	i	• If they recognise her in a restaurant, she gets one of the best/better tables • In the streets people smile at her • Fans ask for her autograph *Any one of the above 3 points for 1 mark*
2	c	ii	• It is difficult to escape • It is difficult not to draw attention to herself • She would like to walk into a shop where the shop attendants did not recognise her *Any one of the above 3 points for 1 mark*

Question			Expected Answer(s)
2	d	i	• Going on holiday • Relaxing on the beach *Any one of the above 2 points for 1 mark*
2	d	ii	• Because she misses her mother's cooking/food • Because she likes to spend time with her family *Any one of the above 2 points for 1 mark*
2	e		• Walking on the beach • Exercising in the gym • Going to a zumba class *Any one of the above 3 points for 1 mark*
2	f		• Has never smoked • Balanced diet • Doesn't eat much fat/fatty food • Tries to sleep for 8 hours *Any two of the above 4 points for 2 marks*
2	g		• She speaks French fluently • She always sings one song in French at her concerts • She wants to improve her English because she thinks languages are important • She likes listening to music in English *Any two of the above 4 points for 2 marks*

Section 2 — Writing

Candidates will write 120–150 words in a piece of extended writing in Spanish addressing a stimulus of three questions in Spanish.

Mark	Content	Accuracy	Language resource: variety, range, structures
10	• The content is comprehensive • The topic is addressed fully, in a balanced way • Some candidates may also provide additional information • Overall this comes over as a competent, well thought-out response to the task which reads naturally	• The language is accurate throughout. However where the candidate attempts to go beyond the range of the task, a slightly higher number of inaccuracies need not detract from the overall very good impression • A comprehensive range of verbs is used accurately and tenses are consistent and accurate • There is evidence of confident handling of all aspects of grammar and spelling accurately, although the language may contain a number of minor errors, or even one serious major error	• The language used is detailed and complex • There is good use of adjectives, adverbs, prepositional phrases and, where appropriate, word order • A comprehensive range of verbs/verb forms, tenses and constructions is used • Some modal verbs and infinitives may be used • The candidate is comfortable with the first person of the verb and generally uses a different verb in each sentence • The candidate uses co-ordinating conjunctions and subordinate clauses throughout the writing • Sentences are mainly complex and accurate • The language flows well
8	• The content is clear • The topic is addressed clearly	• The language is mostly accurate However where the candidate attempts to use detailed and complex language, this may be less successful, although basic structures are used accurately • A range of verbs is used accurately and tenses are generally consistent and accurate • There may be a few errors in spelling, adjective endings and, where relevant, case endings. Use of accents is less secure • Verbs and other parts of speech are used accurately but simply	The language used is detailed and complex • The candidate uses a range of verbs/verb forms and other constructions • There may be less variety in the verbs used • The candidate is comfortable with the first person of the verb and generally uses a different verb in each sentence • Most of the more complex sentences use co-ordinating conjunctions, and there may also be examples of subordinating conjunctions where appropriate • Sentences are generally complex and mainly accurate • At times the language may be more basic than might otherwise be expected at this level • There may be an example of minor misuse of dictionary • Overall the writing will be very competent, essentially correct, but may be pedestrian

Mark	Content	Accuracy	Language resource: variety, range, structures
6	• The content is adequate and may be similar to that of an 8 or a 10 • The topic is addressed adequately	• The language may be mostly accurate. However, in places, control of the language structure may deteriorate significantly • The verbs are generally correct, but basic. Tenses may be inconsistent, with present tenses being used at times instead of past tenses • There may be errors in spelling, e.g. reversal of vowel combinations adjective endings and some prepositions may be inaccurate or omitted, e.g. I went the town There are quite a few errors in other parts of speech — personal pronouns, gender of nouns, adjective endings, cases, singular/plural confusion — and in the use of accents • Overall, there is more correct than incorrect and there is the impression that the candidate can handle tenses	• There are some examples of detailed and complex language • The language is perhaps repetitive and uses a limited range of verbs and fixed phrases not appropriate to this level • The candidate relies on a limited range of vocabulary and structures • There is minimal use of adjectives, probably mainly after "is" • The candidate has a limited knowledge of plurals • The candidate copes with the present tense of most verbs • Where the candidate attempts constructions with modal verbs, these are not always successful • Sentences are mainly single clause and may be brief • There may be some misuse of dictionary
4	• The content may be limited and may be presented as a single paragraph • The topic is addressed in a limited way	• The language used to address the more predictable aspects of the task may be accurate. However, major errors occur when the candidate attempts to address a less predictable aspect • A limited range of verbs is used • Ability to form tenses is inconsistent • In the use of the perfect tense the auxiliary verb is omitted on a number of occasions • There may be confusion between the singular and plural form of verbs • There are errors in many other parts of speech — gender of nouns, cases, singular/plural confusion — and in spelling and, where appropriate, word order • Several errors are serious, perhaps showing mother tongue interference • Overall there is more incorrect than correct	• There is limited use of detailed and complex language and the language is mainly simple and predictable • The language is repetitive, with undue reliance on fixed phrases and a limited range of common basic verbs such as to be, to have, to play, to watch • There is inconsistency in the use of various expressions, especially verbs • Sentences are basic and there may be one sentence that is not intelligible to a sympathetic native speaker • An English word may appear in the writing or a word may be omitted • There may be an example of serious dictionary misuse
2	• The content may be basic or similar to that of a 4 or even a 6 • The topic is thinly addressed	• The language is almost completely inaccurate throughout the writing and there is little control of language structure • Many of the verbs are incorrect or even omitted. There is little evidence of tense control • There are many errors in other parts of speech — personal pronouns, gender of nouns, cases, singular/plural confusion • Prepositions are not used correctly	• There is little use, if any, of detailed and complex language • The candidate has a very limited vocabulary • Verbs used more than once may be written differently on each occasion • The candidate cannot cope with more than one or two basic verbs • Sentences are very short and some sentences may not be understood by a sympathetic native speaker • Several English or "made-up" words may appear in the writing • There are examples of serious dictionary misuse

Mark	Content	Accuracy	Language resource: variety, range, structures
0	• The content is very basic • The candidate is unable to address the topic	• The language is seriously inaccurate throughout the writing and there is almost no control of language structure • (Virtually) nothing is correct • Most of the errors are serious • Very little is intelligible to a sympathetic native speaker	• There is no evidence of detailed and complex language • The candidate copes only with "have" and "am" • There may be several examples of mother tongue interference • Very few words are written correctly in the modern language • English words are used • There may be several examples of serious dictionary misuse

HIGHER SPANISH 2015

Reading

Question		Expected Answer(s)	Max mark
1	a	• To be the first/top/best/number one/ the smartest in the class • To make/keep their parents happy/to please/to satisfy their parents • Because they are fascinated by learning/to learn new things/For the fascination of learning new things/ It is fascinating to learn new things/ Learning new things fascinates them (Must have new things) *Any two of the above 3 points for 2 marks* **Unacceptable answers** To be the best in the school They learn fascinating new things They are fascinated by new things (i.e. the omission of learning) They want to learn new things	2
	b	• Lost in a new/different atmosphere/ environment/surroundings • Overwhelmed/overloaded/with the increased amount of/more/ increased quantity (of school) work/ heavier amount of work/They feel the increased amount (of school) work is too much/They struggle with… *Any one of the above 2 points for 1 mark* **Unacceptable answers** Distinct They feel lost in a new secondary school	1
2		• They feel the need/they need/it is necessary/there is a necessity to be valued/worthy/appreciated • They feel the need to find meaning in what they do/They find what they do meaningful • They want to have/be surrounded by a group/gang of close friends • They want to spend time with them/ dedicate/devote (lots of) time to them/their friends/it *Any two of the above 4 points for 2 marks* **Unacceptable answers** Valuable/price/valuated In what they have/They need to find meaning/regrettable Nearby friends/gang (on its own)/They have a group of friends/They need to make friends/have a gang of friends around them They want to dedicate a lot of time	2

Question		Expected Answer(s)	Max mark
3		• To understand that freedom/liberty brings/involves/comes with/has/ implies responsibilities • (To understand that if they want to make their own decisions), there will be consequences of their decisions/ They will have to deal with/face/ live with/pay the consequences of their own decisions/to make them think about the consequences of their decisions/there will consequences derived from their decisions **Unacceptable answers** The freedom of responsibilities/take the responsibility of freedom They have to cheer up To make decisions (on their own) To make independent decisions Ignore they have to cheer up/brighten their kids to … if the rest of the answer is correct	2
4	a	• They came up against/faced more difficult/very/the most difficult work/ homework/tasks/they found the work more difficult • They became overwhelmed with the work/the work was overwhelming • They (no longer) knew/didn't know how to/couldn't find time (to finish) their work/they didn't have time to finish their work *Any two of the above 3 points for 2 marks* **Unacceptable answers** Chores Difficult work They had to find more time No longer had time to go out *N.B. No penalty for repeated mistranslation of tareas in bullet points 1 and 3*	2
	b	• Start with what you like the least/ don't like much/least favourite/what you prefer the least • Switch/mix/merge/combine/sort between subjects that are more complicated and the ones which are easier **Unacceptable answers** Start with what you don't like/what you like best/better Do less of what you like What you wanted to do Any reference to results *N.B. Study diary/Manage their time is incorrect*	2

Question		Expected Answer(s)	Max mark
5		Re-read lines 31 to 36 According to a recent study, in what ways can teachers also help to motivate their students? State any three things. • Teacher's expectations can have a powerful effect on pupil behaviour • Have high/big expectations/aspirations of their students • (Make sure/Ensure) students participate/take part <u>actively/active</u> participation in class/participants are <u>active</u> in the classroom • Vary teaching methods/the way you teach/use a variety of teaching methods • (Progressively/gradually) increase/raise the difficulty of <u>reading material</u> *Any three of the above 5 points for 3 marks* **Unacceptable answers** From their pupils Participate in classroom activities Change the way you teach Educational methods Lecture material/lessons Increment Make progress in the reading materials	3
6		• An increase/improvement in (academic/school) performance/results/achievement(s) • Pupils know how to/can/are able to/they have learned to develop (their) linguistic/language skills/ability • It gives them confidence/they have confidence/are more confident/it makes them more confident *Any two of the above 3 points for 2 marks* **Unacceptable answers** Academic productivity/efficiency/school's output Pupils know to develop their linguistic skills Pupils are developing/have developed/developed their linguistic skills Linguistic habits Proper Trust	2

Question		Expected Answer(s)	Max mark
7	a	• Because they (already) have everything/all they want • (Because) this/the idea/it bores them/It generates boredom/The idea is boring/tedious *Any one of the above 2 points for 1 mark* **Unacceptable answers** Get everything/anything they want Know everything It is generally boring	1
	b	• (They are studying to learn) to think for themselves/so they can think for themselves/(to learn and) to think for themselves/they have to/must think for themselves • (They must educate/train/shape themselves/must study/learn/) to be useful to society/make themselves useful to society/they must become useful for society/they must develop skills to be useful to society *Any two of the above 3 points for 2 marks* **Unacceptable answers** Learn about yourself	1
8		**Candidates should make at least one assertion which gives the writer's opinion. There should be at least one justification for this assertion.** Illustrative answers • The author thinks that parents and teachers should employ a range of strategies to motivate teenagers. (Assertion) He tells us about Rocío Rodríguez who helped her daughters by suggesting strategies and giving advice on how to cope with their work./He tells us about Paco Bernabéu Martínez who implemented motivational strategies in his classroom. (Justification) • The author's opinion is that there are many strategies to motivate teenagers. (Assertion) He outlines what parents should do to motivate their children./He talks about the findings of a recent study which gives advice to teachers. (Justification) • Overall the writer thinks that it is important to find strategies to motivate teenagers. (Assertion) He gives examples of instances where strategies employed by teachers have had positive results. (Justification)	2

Question 9 – Translation

The translation into English is allocated 10 marks. The text for translation will be divided into a number of sense units. Each sense unit is worth 2 marks, which will be awarded according to the quality and accuracy of the translation into English.

Sense Unit 1	(2 marks)
La falta de atención es otro problema que algunos profesores han observado.	**Lack of attention is another problem which some teachers have noticed.** the/a lack of attention (a) failure to pay attention teachers/several teachers have observed/have seen/ have noted
Sense Unit 2	(2 marks)
Dicen que es cada vez más difícil	**They say it is more and more difficult** It is said that ... It is increasingly difficult It is becoming harder and harder It is becoming more and more difficult It is becoming/getting more and more difficult It is ever more difficult
Sense Unit 3	(2 marks)
conseguir que los adolescentes se concentren en un proyecto escolar.	**to get teenagers to concentrate on a school project.** to make teenagers concentrate ... to get teenagers concentrating on a school project to make sure the teenagers are concentrating to keep teenagers focused on a school project/school work
Sense Unit 4	(2 marks)
Esto es porque están acostumbrados a ver programas de televisión breves,	**This is because they are used to watching short elevision programmes,** They are accustomed to watching ... They will be used to seeing ... television shows brief/short programmes N.B. Accept mis-spelling of "programmes"

Sense Unit 5	(2 marks)
y a usar las redes sociales que requieren un bajo nivel de concentración.	**and using social networks which require a low level of concentration.** a low concentration level a short concentration span and using Social networks requiring a low level of concentration social media low levels of concentration

Directed Writing

Please refer back to pages 88–90 for further advice on the General Marking Principles for Directed Writing.

Section 1 – Listening

Item 1

Question			Expected Answer(s)	Max mark
1	a		• (She) likes/is interested in science/ maths. She has always liked….. • She likes seeing how things work • She wants to work using her scientific knowledge *Any one of the above 3 points for 1 mark* **Unacceptable answers** Good at ... ... are her favourite subjects	1
1	b	i	• It has an international reputation/it is internationally/universally/famous/ recognised/acclaimed/renowned Known around the world **Unacceptable answers** "Good reputation" with no mention of "international" International university	1
1	b	ii	• She wants to live/stay in/share/rent a flat with her (best) friend(s) • She wants to be away/far/move away from her parents *Any one of the above 2 points for 1 mark* **Unacceptable answers** Be/live with her friends with no mention of "flat" Live on her own/wants her own flat Buy a flat	1

Question			Expected Answer(s)	Max mark
1	b	iii	• Be(come) independent/have independence/gain independence • Live within her (own) means/gets by on her own/manages on her own *Any one of the above 2 points for 1 mark* *N.B. Live independently = 1 mark* **Unacceptable answers** Learn independently Live on her own/by herself	1
1	c		• Be hardworking/a hard worker/dedicated to work • (Be able to) work in a team/group/Be good in a team/collaborate as part of a team/team work • Leadership *Any two of the above 3 points for 2 marks* **Unacceptable answers** Manage a team/talk to people/capable of talking to people in a group	2
1	d		• Because there are job offers in <u>other countries</u>/There are opportunities to work in <u>other countries</u>/There are jobs <u>abroad</u>/She is/will be able to work/get a job/<u>abroad</u> • Because she would love to/wants to <u>live abroad</u> (for a year)/spend time (a year) in another country *Any one of the above 2 points for 1 mark* **Unacceptable answers** ... other places	1
1	e		• 'She is confident about her skills'.	1

Item 2

Question	Expected Answer(s)	Max mark
2 a	• He was interested in theatre/drama as a child/He has always been interested in/liked the theatre • He was a member of/in the (school) cinema/film club • (He decided to) study/studied drama/acting/it at university. (Ignore 'art' as in 'he studied art and drama) • He got a job in television *Any two of the above 4 points for 2 marks* **Unacceptable answers** He was interested in theatre/drama Made a cinema club Went to a club Attended drama club Studied "Arts" on its own	2

Question			Expected Answer(s)	Max mark
2	b	i	• He was behind the cameras/working with cameras/camera man/behind the scenes **Unacceptable answers** In front of Cameras (on its own)	1
2	b	ii	• He learned (a lot)/got advice <u>from</u> the other actors/colleagues/learned off actors **Unacceptable answers** Learned <u>about</u> the other actors Worked with other actors Got to know lots of other actors Learned of	1
2	c		• He has breakfast with the team/film crew • He reads/checks messages/notes/letters/from fans/fan mail • Reads/checks/news of family/friends on social networks • Gets updates on/talks/replies to family/friends on social media • Learn/memorise his lines/script *Any two of the above 5 points for 2 marks* **Unacceptable answers** He makes breakfast He has breakfast He sends/replies messages to his fans *N.B. Arrives at studio at 8 to start at 8.30 = 0 mark*	2
2	d		• He spends time with his wife/son/kid/child • He goes (out) for lunch/something to eat/dinner with friends (in the old area of town) • He goes for walks along/on/goes down the beach *Any two of the above 3 points for 2 marks* **Unacceptable answers** Daughter Goes/walk to the beach	2
2	e		• Focus on cinema/film projects/do more cinematic projects/appear in films/do films/be in a film/be in more films • Work on stories/plots that have a (social) message • Travel/visit see the world with his family *Any two of the above 3 points for 2 marks* **Unacceptable answers** Photography Star Write stories	2

Question			Expected Answer(s)	Max mark
2	f		• people want to watch something on television/people will always watch TV/people want something onTV • (people want) to escape from reality (for a moment)/helps to escape from daily life • (people want) to be informed/for information/to be up to date with info • (people want) to laugh • They will continue to produce programmes/series *Any two of the above 5 points for 2 marks* **Unacceptable answers** People always want to watch more To relax Movies/films	2

Section 2 — Writing

Please see pages 91–93 for General Marking Principles for Writing.

HIGHER SPANISH 2016

Section 1 — Reading

Question			Expected Answer(s)	Max mark
1			• Lack of economic resources/money • Desire to be (more) creative with ingredients **Unacceptable answers:** Lack of food resource Fault/flaw/absence Insufficient funds/resources The crash/economic crisis Want/to have more creative ingredients	2
2	a		• 86% of food thrown out is from leftovers/excess/scraps	1
	b		• (Consumer) habits have changed/ modified • (Consumers) have reduced the amount of food that goes in the bin • And they reuse/re-utilise (more frequent/frequently) products (like oil) **Unacceptable answers:** Customs/modificated Junk food	3
3			• It could have been eaten/ consumed if people had only bought what they needed **Unacceptable answers:** When they need it	1
4	a		• Save some money for spending on their children/children's expenses/costs **Unacceptable answers:** Save money for children Give money to the children For the children to spend	1
	b		• They think about/take into consideration/bear in mind /take into account who will be at home each afternoon/evening/night • They only cook enough/sufficient for them • They freeze left over/excess food (to use it in following days) **Unacceptable answers:** Count/they know who/have a check/ calculate/keep track For themselves	3

Question			Expected Answer(s)	Max mark
5	a		• To cook with creativity/cook creatively	1
	b		• They cooked/made a different international dish/plate for each/every day of the week • (Every/each person) they made/created/think up/thought up a series of recipes • They make sure/ensure the food was healthy, balanced and low calorie/little/few calories **Unacceptable answers:** Meal Each day for a week/Each day of the week Think of	2
	c		• To combine culinary traditions/traditional dishes cooking with the demands of modern life/day **Unacceptable answers:** Culinaries To change/match Modern world	1
6			• Compare prices in the nearest/closer/closest/nearby/local supermarkets • Save up to/as much as/as far as 40% by scanning the bar codes • Enter/put/put in/insert fridge ingredients and the app suggests a range of possible dishes **Unacceptable answers:** Compare more closely At least/almost/nearly Want (you tell the fridge what you want)	3

Question			Expected Answer(s)	Max mark
7			Award 1 mark for making an assertion. And 1 mark for making at least one justification. It can be done in a number of ways: e.g. The writer thinks it is easy/not easy to reduce food waste = Assertion Possible justifications, which would not contradict the gist of the text • People can be creative in their cooking • People can go to classes to learn ways of cooking • They can learn traditional ways of cooking using leftovers • People are having to make a lot of effort, e.g. cooking classes, planning meals, workshops are available • They can set themselves rules • They can use technology • They can share a meal with others around a table If justifications are given in Spanish, candidate needs to explain/say what they mean in English/and how they work for their choice of justification.	2
8			**Translate into English:** "Otra solución . . . restaurante cercano" (lines 21–24). **Translation** Otra solución que podría reducir el desperdicio **another solution that could reduce waste** es compartir una comida casera alrededor de la mesa. **is sharing a home-cooked meal around the table** Por desgracia, debido al ritmo de trabajo, reuniones y demás compromisos diarios, **Unfortunately due to the pace of work, work meetings and other daily commitments,** comer en casa con la familia o los amigos se limita normalmente a los fines de semana. **eating at home with family or friends is normally limited to weekends.** Para los demás días, existe la opción de salir a cenar a un restaurante cercano. **For the other days there is the option of going out for dinner in a nearby restaurant.**	10

Question 9 – Translation

The translation into English is allocated 10 marks. The text for translation will be divided into a number of sense units. Each sense unit is worth 2 marks, which will be awarded according to the quality and accuracy of the translation into English.

Unit 1	*(2 marks)*
Otra solución que podría reducir el desperdicio	another solution that could/might/would be able to reduce waste/the waste/wastage
Unit 2	*(2 marks)*
es compartir una comida casera alrededor de la mesa.	is sharing/by sharing a home cooked/homemade meal around the table/at the table is to share home cooking home cooked food/lunch
Unit 3	*(2 marks)*
Por desgracia, debido al ritmo de trabajo, reuniones y demás compromisos diarios,	Unfortunately due to pace of work/work pattern/work routines, meetings and other daily commitments/engagements, social gatherings (instead of meetings)
Unit 4	*(2 marks)*
comer en casa con la familia o los amigos se limita normalmente a los fines de semana.	eating at home/to eat at home with family or friends is normally limited to weekends.
Unit 5	*(2 marks)*
Para los demás días, existe la opción de salir a cenar a un restaurante cercano.	For/on the other days/as for the other days/there is/there exists the option of going/to go out for dinner/tea/supper in a nearby restaurant.

Directed Writing

Please refer back to pages 88–90 for further advice on the General Marking Principles for Directed Writing.

Section 1 – Listening

Item 1

Question		Expected Answer(s)	Max mark
1	a	6 weeks	1
	b	• Leadership (skills) • Communication (skills) • Teamwork (Any 2 from 3) **Unacceptable answers:** Group work Working with others	2
	c	• Loves/likes nature • Loves/likes being in the fresh air/outside • They helped/supported each other (Any 1 from 3) **Unacceptable answers:** Nature Naturalness He saw nature Got to experience nature He spent time outside The views were lovely	1
	d	• (He could not stand) the cold water • He's used to the Mediterranean climate (Any 1 from 2) **Unacceptable answers:** It was cold The weather was cold	1
	e	(That there are many) words/expressions that are (only) used in Scotland/There are Scottish words/expressions **Unacceptable answers:** He used expressions in Scotland	1
	f	(He's applied for a job as) a camp instructor in Spain **Unacceptable answers:** Any other country Visit a camp in Spain	1
	g	He has benefited from the trip	1

Item 2

Question			Expected Answer(s)	Max mark
2	a		• She's good/great at maths • She wants to know (more) about/learn about/find out about different/other cultures /likes learning about other cultures **Unacceptable answers:** She likes Maths She is good at it Distinctive culture Distinct cultures She likes other cultures She knows a lot about culture She has learned a lot studying two languages	2
	b		• Recently built/a new build • It is on the outskirts (of the town where she lives) • Very spacious • A whole floor for technology/ good technology facilities/part of the school is dedicated to technology/technology suite • Great sports pitches/facilities/ grounds/fields • Well-equipped/modern gym • Good reputation for sport/ famous for sport **(Any 3)** **Unacceptable answers:** Reconstructed School is modern In the town where she lives It is dedicated to technology It has new technology Hall Camps PE department Clubs Good reputation	3
	c		• Interactive activities on the (smart) board • Grammar (exercises) • Read magazines/read about other countries **(Any 2 from 3)** **Unacceptable answers:** Interactive lessons Newspapers Books Learn about other countries	2

Question			Expected Answer(s)	Max mark
	d	i	• Very strict • (They complain that) they don't let pupils talk (in class) • Teachers are fair **(Any 2 from 3)** **Unacceptable answers:** Too strict They do not speak in class They moan a lot	2
		ii	• The teachers demand/expect a lot in terms of quality of work/school work/a high quality of work • More relaxed atmosphere/ environment • The teachers give us/we get/we have (much) more responsibility **(Any 2 from 3)** **Unacceptable answers:** Teachers expect more work It is more relaxed They are more relaxed It is more relaxing There is a better atmosphere Very relaxed She is more responsible The teachers give us a lot of responsibility *Teachers are fair	2
	e		Set up/open/have her own business/company/shop **Unacceptable answers:** Work for a business	1

Section 2 – Writing

Please see pages 91–93 for General Marking Principles for Writing.

Acknowledgements

To Come